Mablethorpe

in old picture postcards

by
David Cuppleditch

European Library - Zaltbommel/Netherlands MCMLXXXV

To Alexandra, my daughter

Acknowledgments:
I would like to thank Charles Smith, Norman Cawkwell, Mrs. S.M.C. Vamplew, Chris Birchmore and Peter Chambers for lending me certain postcards used in this book. A special thanks goes yet again to Ken Atterby and I am particularly grateful to Peter Chambers who not only supplied much of the information used in this volume but also checked my manuscript carefully.

Cover picture:
Mablethorpe sands circa 1902.

GB   ISBN 90 288 3036 7 / CIP

European Library in Zaltbommel/Netherlands publishes among other things the following series:

IN OLD PICTURE POSTCARDS *is a series of books which sets out to show what a particular place looked like and what life was like in Victorian and Edwardian times. A book about virtually every town in the United Kingdom is to be published in this series. By the end of this year about 175 different volumes will have appeared. 1,250 books have already been published devoted to the Netherlands with the title* **In oude ansichten.** *In Germany, Austria and Switzerland 500, 60 and 15 books have been published as* **In alten Ansichten;** *in France by the name* **En cartes postales anciennes** *and in Belgium as* **En cartes postales anciennes** *and/or* **In oude prentkaarten** *150 respectively 400 volumes have been published.*

For further particulars about published or forthcoming books, apply to your bookseller or direct to the publisher.

This edition has been printed and bound by Grafisch Bedrijf De Steigerpoort in Zaltbommel/Netherlands.

INTRODUCTION

Assembling this set of old picture postcards has been rather like gathering enough material for a magic lantern show. As each card unfolds a part of history comes to life and shows the development of Mablethorpe as a town. The comments on the reverse sides of these postcards (which I personally find most interesting) depict a seaside resort that has experienced just as much inclement weather as it has sunshine.

As far as I know there has never been a book on Mablethorpe apart from a photographic study produced in 1905 and a deluge of tourist brochures which have been used for advertising the town. In a Victorian guide book Mablethorpe was described as *the smallest and most primitive looking of all the resorts along the Lincolnshire coastline... a country village with comfortable and cosy hotels and good lodging accommodation.* Over the years this small country village has become a town which seems to have been put together in a somewhat haphazard fashion.

Of course during that time Mablethorpe has seen an assortment of characters flow through the town. The oddest of which was Emerald Watson who was better known simply as 'Emerald'. With no fixed abode he spent his time drifting between Alford, Louth and Mablethorpe and tramped along his merry way dressed in rubber thigh boots, a floppy hat and an assortment of multifarious overcoats. The son of a country parson Emerald enjoyed the life of a vagrant or to be more polite – 'a knight of the road'. Free from rates, taxes and those 'little household bothers' that beset all of us, he was a well-known figure at cattle markets or on Mablethorpe beach where he found odd jobs. For in his lifetime he never begged at all but as one reporter was to comment ...*if you particularly wanted to give him a present he would take it and thank you with his small cheerful smile!*

Another memorable character is Dallas Denton-Cox who looks after the donkeys on the beach. His mother lived in the Boulevard and (for a while) ran the local Lyric Cinema, but Denton-Cox is no ordinary donkey man. His pro forma is littered with degrees and qualifications and he even interpreted for the BBC but despite this he prefers to look after the donkeys on Mablethorpe sands.

Miss Francis on the other hand who lived in Church Lane was a very odd fish. Mostly dressed in brown overalls it appeared that she earned her living by helping out in other people's gardens because she would frequently be seen about the town with gardening gear stuffed into an old pram. On Sundays she would dress up in black and was extremely religious. However, the house that she lived in was something of a cattery and her pets gradually took over her home. This was somewhat alarming to her neighbours and I would imagine that the smell can't have been very pleasant either! She also used to hang decapitated goats heads on the eaves of her bungalow but quite why, no one has been able to ascertain.

There has however, been a more notable side to Mablethorpe's recent history. For example few people realise that Billy Butlin, who went on to build up the enormous Butlin holiday complex, actually started his career with a hoop-la stand on Mablethorpe beach. He lodged in a house on the corner of Waterloo Road with High Street (where W.H. Brown's, the estate agents, are now) and the Butlin association was to last until the 1960's when they left Mablethorpe for good. Also the father of that ever popular magician Paul Daniels was a humble projectionist at the old Victoria Cinema – and a second projectionist at that! But the one star who has never forgotten his associations with the town is Bill Owen (or 'Compo' out of 'Last of the Summer Wine') who spent much of his early life in Mablethorpe and has frequently referred to the town in numerous TV and radio broadcasts. Many popular personalities have been invited to turn on the town's illuminations each year. In recent times such celebrities as David Hamilton (the disc jockey), Ken Dodd, Tommy Trinder and Ivy Tinsley (the actress in Coronation Street) have all performed their duties admirably.

It is difficult to believe that as far back as 1887 a Mrs. Benson agreed to underwrite the building of a pier off Mablethorpe beach. Mrs. Benson lived in Utterby House on the corner of High Street with Gibraltar Road, which was later converted into the Café Regent. The pier would have been sixty yards long and tenders were invited to be handed in to the Book-in-Hand Hotel by interested contractors. However, the scheme was obviously abandoned and like so many high-faluting ideas it was simply shelved. Had the plan gone ahead I've no doubt the town would have benefitted greatly. Even so to most small children the name of Mablethorpe is synonymous with donkey rides, sandcastles and paddling pools. But there is a more serious side to the town's history and well being. The submarine forests (only the stumps are visible these days) which can be seen at the lowest ebb of the spring tide are a constant reminder that nowhere is safe on this ever shifting coastline; a fact which none of us ought to forget! Through the ages Mablethorpe has been invaded several times. In the sixteenth and seventeenth centuries Dutch pirates frequently ransacked the town and these little capers (Dutch pirate ships) were feared by the local people. During Cromwell's Civil War, Mablethorpe Hall (now an old people's home) played an important part as a Royalist garrison. It had been the home of the Fitzwilliam family whose founder was Marshall of William the Conqueror's army at Hastings. Many of their monuments now lie in St. Mary's Church. But eventually Mablethorpe Hall succumbed to that pious butcher Cromwell and it was overrun by the Roundheads.

More recently photographers have invaded the town on a much more friendly basis. Although many have been amateurs, Mablethorpe was fortunate to escape from the street photographers of the fifties and sixties who were usually spivs or con-men touting their instant 'walking pictures'. (This was in the age before the polaroid camera.) Their photographs only lasted a few hours before fading in the sun and left a nicotine-type stain on your fingers. Like their wares most of these street photographers have faded into oblivion. Of the other more respectable photographers probably the best known was Nainby, the Victorian photographer. Another profilic cameraman was A. James of Louth who took a few Mablethorpe studies before the First World War. In the 1918-1945 period F. Soar did much work although Wrates from Skegness also took a few photos and undoubtedly the main Mablethorpe photographer in the period after 1948 was D. Camm. Without the photographer's eagle eye, this slim volume could not have been devised.

1. In the middle of the nineteenth century Mablethorpe was just another sleepy back-water village with little of note and little or no reason for anyone to want to go there. One of its more unique features was a restaurant known as the 'Pie in Hand' which opened in 1875 and served pork pies and cups of tea at one shilling per person. The name came from the figurehead of a stranded barge called the 'Rennata'. This was placed, with the addition of a wooden pork pie in her hand, on to the front of the building in 1878. It can be seen here as the small white figure half way down the street on the right.

MABLETHORPE, TENNYSON'S LODGINGS   53670

2. It was to Mablethorpe that the young Alfred Tennyson came for peace and quiet. Together with his brother Charles they retired to this part of the coast on that famous day in 1827 when their first published work entitled 'Poems by Two Brothers' came out; roaming amongst the sand dunes and declaiming verses to the empty sandhills.

TENNYSON'S SEA SIDE LODGINGS, MABLETHORPE.

3. The young Tennyson children frequently journeyed to these lodgings with their parents for their annual summer break. Known locally as Ingoldby House it is hidden behind some houses in Quebec Road. But Alfred was to return here as a young man and on one occasion wrote to 'Dear Old Fitz' (the Fitzgerald of Omar Khayyam fame): *Mablethorpe, near Alford, is the place where I am. I walk about the coast and have it all to myself, sand and sea.*

Convalescent Home, Mablethorpe. J 5964. (*Jagger's Series.*)

4. Because of the fresh air and quiet surroundings the convalescent home was built and completed in June 1871 at a cost of £3,800. It was designed by Mr. James Fowler of Louth and the idea of the home originated from a Miss Emily Anderson who saw the need to provide holidays for the underprivileged and those recuperating from non-infectious diseases in the Midland counties. Canon Pretyman, a wealthy clergyman from Great Carlton, put up much of the money and over the years this home has given help to countless hundreds of people.

4843. CONVALESCENT HOME MABLETHORPE

5. In 1900 the inmates were expected to contribute 4/= per week towards the cost of their stay and pay their own rail fares to and from the institution. There was accommodation for thirty men and thirty women and 'sea baths' (hot or cold) could be had at a small cost on application to the matron. The bath house can be seen to the right of this postcard — it is the small separate building. At present the convalescent home is up for sale and despite its cold, hard looking Victorian exterior it is surprisingly clean and comfortable inside.

6. A children's wing was added in 1907 which allowed for a further ten boys and ten girls to stay at the home. The wing was officially opened by Baroness Von Eckardstein, who was connected to the Maples family of Maples Furniture fame. The third clergyman from the right is Bishop Edward King, who looks as if he is giving his blessing to the whole proceedings.

S 11150   G. N. RLY STATION, MABLETHORPE.

7. However, with the advent of the railway things were to change dramatically. Originally known as the 'Louth and East Coast Railway' this stretch of line was opened on 16th October 1877. It brought with it a flood of visitors to this part of the coast and set the seal on the pre-war boom for Mablethorpe.

8. Posters soon adorned the railway hoardings and this one is particularly notable. Everything that Mablethorpe had to offer summer visitors is clearly marked. In the centre picture the two striped huts to the side of the Basin belonged to A. James, photographer.

S 5719   WESLEYAN CHAPEL, MABLETHORPE.

9. In the middle distance of this postcard is the old railway footbridge which used to have ornate Art Nouveau hand rails on the top of it. Sadly, this has been demolished but the Wesleyan Chapel on the left still stands and was converted into a printing works for a time but is now a warehouse.

91. 101. High St from the Pullover. Mablethorpe.

10. Just after the arrival of the railway, the Pullover, the main pathway to the sea, was laid with railway sleepers and then covered with concrete in a design reminiscent of a bar of Cadbury's chocolate. The gap between the sand dunes was called the Pullover because it was at this spot that local people could 'pull over' the provisions and imported goods which arrived on the shore.

S 8304   THE BOOTHS MABLETHORPE BEACH

11. A series of booths were hastily erected on the sands, hiring out deck chairs at two pence per day (a grossly inflated price even for the 1890's) and selling ice-cream. Clearly visible is the sign which says 'Ices Warranted Pure' an important consideration in the days when typhoid was rampant throughout the country.

View of Beach, Mablethorpe

12. The chief attractions of this resort were the rolling sandhills, open beaches and fresh air. Tacky gentility could roam along the sands and ponder their own self importance without disturbing anyone. The one noticeable part of this postcard is the Outfall; it can be seen here as the long circular pipe reminiscent of a groyne in the middle distance. The Outfall drains all the surrounding agricultural land of surplus water and takes it out into the North Sea. In fact it is still there today and is prominent because of the small boxes that sit on top of it which are simply air vents.

IN THE SHADE
AT MABLETHORPE.

It's very Hot down here.
A Little Shade is quite
a boon.

13. Of course seaside trinkets were put on sale and amongst them was the inevitable postcard. Small shops and bazaars were stocked to the gunwales with seaside views. It is difficult to believe that this particular card was once considered 'naughty'! The sand dunes offered an ideal retreat for young courting couples but in the light of our permissive society this card seems extremely tame.

IT IS NO
CRIME
TO KISS, IN
MABLETHORPE.

"To Err is human, to kiss, divine"

14. Yet another nostalgic card from that golden era which is just as risque as the last. It was addressed to a Miss White of Candlesby Rectory, Burgh, and says: *My dearest, as you see it is no crime to kiss at Mable-thorpe, and it will be no crime for us to kiss at Candlesby. So please meet at 9.15 tomorrow night,* and it is signed XYZ which presumably meant that the sender wished to remain anonymous.

VIEWS of MABLETHORPE

PROMENADE & SHELTERS

SANDHILLS AND NORTH SANDS

PARISH CHURCH

SANDS

CALM SEA

15. It was much more common for people to send general view cards like this. Usually accompanied by trite messages such as 'Wish you were here' or 'Having a lovely time' these cards were once sent in their thousands yet strangely are difficult to find today.

16. Mablethorpe's great threat has always been the sea and many small boats and swimmers have been thankful for the lifeboat. In 1883 Mr. Heywood Lonsdale presented the Heywood Lifeboat to the town. Of the crew, dressed in old cork lifebelts, Vickers, Leake, Billy Hunter, Charles Grey, Dales, Horton and Gooding can be seen in this photograph.

17. However, even a lifeboat only has a limited existence and in 1905 Baroness Von Eckardstein named the new lifeboat 'John Rowson Lingard' when the 'Heywood' had served its useful purpose. She is pictured here at the ceremony with Sir Archibald Weigall who was a Member of Parliament for Horncastle.

S 12250　　　　　LAUNCH OF THE LIFEBOAT, MABLETHORPE.

18. It was no mean task to launch a lifeboat at the turn of the century even in fine weather and this postcard depicts just such a scene. Probably a practise run it is obvious that plenty of horses, pulleys and muscle were needed to take the boat into the water and out again. But what I find so fascinating about this card are the wooden boards around the wheels of the boat transporter. Caterpillar tracks had not yet been invented!

A.32554. MABLETHORPE BEACH.

19. In the top left of this postcard is the wreck of the 'Stavanger'. Shortly after it was beached this boat was hauled up on to the sands and converted into a museum; the tops of the masts were cut off and a gang-plank placed into the side of the hulk which allowed visitors easy access. This was quite a novelty sporting such items as pickled mermaids in jars and Neptunes trident. The timbers from wrecks found along this shore were frequently scavenged and used to erect buildings such as the Prussion Queen at Saltfleetby, John Robinson's kitchen in Theddlethorpe Hall and Trusthorpe Post Office.

View of Beach, Mablethorpe

20. To begin with Victorian bathing machines were posted along the beach. These were large and cumbersome and frequently got stuck in the sand and often required cart-horses to pull them out. (On occasions it had been known for one or more of these heavy waggons to float out to sea on a high tide!) They can be seen on the extreme left of this postcard.

S 5707   SANDHILLS & NORTH SANDS, MABLETHORPE.

21. Bell tents soon replaced these bathing machines — they were light, easily manouvre-
able and roomy — in fact during the First World War 26 men could crowd into one of
these bell tents to sleep, the rule being one man per panel of canvas and toes to the pole!

Sea Hills . Mablethorpe.

22. Families could hire out these bell tents for the day, which allowed them to change into their swimsuits discreetly. There is no doubt that these were the forerunners of the beach hut as we know it today.

SOUTH SHORE TENTS
MABLETHORPE

23. In 1905 J. Salmon of Sevenoaks (the well-known postcard publisher) commissioned the artist A.R. Quinton to make a few watercolour sketches of Mablethorpe. The result was a charming set of which this is just one; others include the sands (looking south), Parade and War Memorial, steps and sands (with donkeys), bathing tents — north shore and steps and sands (looking out to sea). Alfred Robert Quinton (1853-1934) was a prolific postcard artist who produced over 2,300 water colours for postcards in total, and for the most part he was paid £4 a piece for each one.

MABLETHORPE RINK.

24. An unusual attraction was the Mablethorpe Rink which was not as you might suspect for ice-skating but for the new-fangled fad of roller-skating! The rink stood off Wellington Road with an entrance in High Street on what is now Fred's Bingo. Basically it comprised of a large tent with gas lighting and a hard wooden floor and it was not uncommon for unsuspecting skaters to have the odd mishap!

A well known resident of Mablethorpe, 59 years of age, weighs 9 stone 6½ lbs, stands 4 feet high.

25. The cheerful little man in this postcard was Hedley Broddle. Standing by the back door of Field View Farm he is still remembered as being quite a character. Employed as a milkman by Mr. William Codd, he would trundle his barrow round the streets of Mablethorpe and ladle out pints of milk from the churn on his hand-cart. After his milk round he would sometimes supplement his income by cleaning knives.

26. Another popular event which ran successfully up to the First World War was the 'Battle of Flowers'. Floats decorated with flowers would parade through the streets and it also gave some people a chance to dress up. Sadly this festival was discontinued after the war and was only revived in the thirties when it became known as Mablethorpe's Carnival, which still takes place today. On the extreme left of this card is Freeman's Family Butchers which is now Queens Arcade.

27. Initially a set of swing-boats was erected to the right hand side of the Pullover as entertainment for children and the young at heart. It is pictured here just to the right of the Pavilion and appears to be being 'set up' for the season. Both the amusements and the booths were taken down in winter.

MABLETHORPE 244

28. Just beyond the swing-boats was Carlton's Cosy Corner where entertainers would give all sorts of renditions to amuse the summer visitors. It was, if you like, a sort of open air old time music hall setting, by the sea.

29. At first these seaside frolics were organised by Dan Idle (seen here) but he was soon replaced by the Clements Brothers. The Clements Pierrots upgraded the standards set by Dan Idle and proved to be even more popular. Although Londoners by birth the Clements Brothers namely Fred, Bob and Jack started their seaside entertainments business in Skegness in 1902, after moving up to Lincolnshire. They extended their family show to Mablethorpe in 1906.

"Clement's Entertainers"

30. Many people can remember the Clements with affection. They gave two day time concerts and one in the evening in the Victoria Road Pavillion. Pictured here are (from top, anti clockwise) Jack Morris (whose real name was Pearce), J. Clements' daughter, the ventriloquist Joe Cookson, Miss Clifford, Leo Christo, an unknown girl entertainer, the baritone Fred Clifford, another unknown girl and in the centre of the group G. Thompson. When the Clements disbanded in the thirties their pavilion was converted into the Victoria Cinema (it is now Grayscroft Coach-park).

31. Clements' fame must have been widespread judging by the size of this crowd!

CLEMENTS
APPEAR HERE 11·30 & 2·45
VICTORIA GARDENS AT 7·45

CLEMENTS.
IN THE EVENT
OF WET WEATHER
ALL CONCE

32. Continuing with the beach entertainments, a helter-skelter was erected next door to the Clements booth. This looks most peculiar without its top! Nevertheless undeterred enthusiasts still clambered up the inside of the frame and jumped on the spiral run. Just to the right of the helter-skelter was an even more precarious device known as the Aerial Flight (the poles can just be seen to the right of the postcard).

The Sands, Mablethorpe.

33. This bizarre system comprised of a rope, pulley and plenty of ambitious young dare-devils who were prepared to sling themselves into mid-air, just for the thrill of it; they hung on to the handles and slid down the rope to a safety net at the bottom but it is unrecorded whether there were any accidents or not. I suppose the sand would act as some sort of buffer to those who lost their grip.

Beach from Sandhills, Mablethorpe

34. By 1910 this helter-skelter had at last received its top! It was not uncommon for children to receive the odd splinter or two on their descent of the spiral even though they slid down on mats.

A 40769. MABLETHORPE: HIGH STREET.

35. On the left of this postcard was the Book-in-Hand Hotel which was built in the early part of the nineteenth century and derived its curious name from a wooden arm which used to protrude from the front of the building holding an open book. Just opposite this (with the ornate iron balcony) was the Louth Hotel. Built in 1878 from designs by Mr. Wallis of Louth, who was better known as a woodcarver, it charged forty shillings per week 'all in' in 1901.

36. The third hotel was the Eagle in Victoria Road which is hardly recogniseable today from the grand edifice which was put up in 1870. It was slightly cheaper than the Louth Hotel and only charged its residents thirty-five shillings a week in 1901. Designed as a high building to give guests a good view of the sea, it was built to meet the expected demand for accommodation occasioned by the new railway.

Victoria Road, Mablethorpe

37. This view of the Eagle will be more familiar to people today. The hotel was named after the eagle which stood on the gable end of the south wing (seen in the previous card).

MABLETHORPE. VICTORIA ROAD.

38. This was the view down Victoria Road from the High Street end. Smithson's Stores on the immediate left sold sand-shoes, bathing drawers, hats and caps and boasted a circulating library.

S 8703   HIGH STREET. MABLETHORPE.

39. There was another lending library at the Post Office, run by Mr. Lewington. There were two good banks namely, the Stamford, Spalding and Boston Bank and the Lincoln and Lindsey Bank where people could readily draw cash. Sharpes Newsagents on the corner of Waterloo Road and High Street (seen here on the left) provided a selection of fancy goods, postcards and periodicals.

Pavilion and Sands, Mablethorpe.

40. Meanwhile the helter-skelter proved to be so popular that another one had to be built to cope with demand. In the centre of the card is an ice-cream booth which was run by Clarke's of Queen Street, Louth.

Swimming Basin, Mablethorpe

41. The swimming basin has long since disappeared together with Professor Hobson Bocock who used to give daily swimming lessons. A later attraction was the one legged diver, Bernard Arthur Pykett who lost his leg in the First World War. He used to perform diving feats into the Basin despite his handicap and Tommy Handley's famous ITMA catch phrase 'Don't Forget the diver!' was attributed to Bernie Pykett when Handley saw him perform off Brighton Pier in Liverpool.

Messrs. Mrs. Bocock and other Swimmers, Mablethorpe

42. Long before the safety council started spending a fortune on adverts to remind people 'to learn to swim' Professor Bocock advocated it as common sense. He is pictured here together with his daughter who taught the 'ladies' outside their changing hut on the sands.

A. 35431. MABLETHORPE PARISH CHURCH.

43. St. Mary's Church was built around 1300. Nestling neatly on the corner of Church Lane and Church Road it stands safely away from the sea. This charming church which has a chancel roof higher than its tower has undergone several restorations including one recently when fifty thousand pounds was raised to restore it. When this photograph was taken there were virtually no houses to be seen whereas today the church is hemmed in between bungalows and semis.

4994 VICTORIA ROAD, MABLETHORPE.

44. The tranquility of Mablethorpe was smashed during the First World War. The convalescent home was lent to the government and converted into a military recuperation centre and Clement's Pavillion in Victoria Road was used as a drill hall for the volunteers.

3712 PARADE & WAR MEMORIAL. MABLETHORPE

45. The War Memorial testifies to Mablethorpe's sacrifice. Built on the north side of the Pullover it faces out to sea.

5029. HIGH STREET, MABLETHORPE.

46. After the war Mablethorpe began to pick up the pieces. This was the view looking down High Street and in comparison to illustration No. 11 the Café Regent on the left has replaced the earlier private house. This café was run by the able Mrs. Parrott who had achieved some recognition from her booth on the sands and had opted for warmer quarters. Many people can still remember her cream teas with relish. She died in 1945 having been in business for fifty years and the café is now a fish and chip shop.

The Model Railway Mablethorpe.

47. One of the chief attractions for children was this model railway which, at this time, was the smallest working model train in *use* in England. Negotiating a circular track of seven and a quarter inch gauge, it went through a series of tunnels, bridges, viaducts and working signals. The proprietors proudly announced their special offer of 'Any lady of 18 stone or more can have a free ride!' But I am not sure whether anyone took this offer up.

48. Another shot of the model railway along the north shore where an interesting item is the First World War pill-box. This postcard would have been taken in 1928/29 when the railway was owned by Bollington and Shaw (seen here). It moved to High Street in about 1930 and was eventually bought by Percy Harding-Kiff, and continued to function up until the Second World War.

Fulbeck House, Mablethorpe

49. Fulbeck House was built circa 1860 when the house only consisted of the right hand side of the building shown in this postcard. The Reverend 'Tommy' Smith, a parson from Fulbeck, lived there; the Art Deco extension was added on to the left hand side in the twenties. It was then known as the Fulbeck Hotel and was still functioning as late as the 1970's when it was demolished altogether and a modern box-structured building, known as 'The Fulbeck' pub put up in its place. Just visible in the bottom left hand corner is a section of the Basin which was 'filled in' in 1939.

ON THE DONKEYS AT MABLETHORPE

50. Looking back at the women's fashions of the twenties it is interesting to note that these same styles seem to be enjoying something of a revival today — the lady in the centre left seems to be wearing culottes? Not so as far as the boys and young men are concerned — I doubt whether short trousers of that length will ever see the light of day again or at least certainly not in a serious capacity, although the short haircuts are a bit reminiscent of 'punk' crew-cuts.

The Kiddies Delight
The Donkeys on the Sands at Mablethorpe.

Empire View. 021.59.

51. 'Oh! I do like to be beside the seaside!' is written all over these young girls' faces. Straddling the donkeys, these girls had their picture taken at what was known as 'Kiddies Corner' (with Clement's Booth in the far distance).

"Kiddies corner"
On the Sands at Mablethorpe.

"Empire View." 021·33.

52. In this postcard taken circa 1932/33 from more or less the same spot as the last, the Clement's Booth in the distance has been taken over by Arthur Sherwin.

53. One of the carefree activities typical of the twenties was a 'round the seaside resorts' trip as a piece of publicity for Raleigh motorcycles. The dashing lady motorcyclist (second bike from the left) was Majorie Cottle and this group stopped off briefly in Mablethorpe on their joyride around the coast. This photograph was taken in George Street when the building on the right was known as Graves' Garage which was later St. Georges Theatre, then the Lyric Cinema and is now the Lyric Bingo Parlour.

54. Another extraordinary piece of publicity in the twenties was a cricket match held on the sands. It was either the largest cricket match ever played or with the largest bats ever used and the proceeds went to the Red Cross. This photograph was taken by A. Howe.

55. Of course Clement's entertainers inspired a host of imitators. Both Chris King and his little helper Joyce (seen here) worked on a booth on the north shore and when this postcard was taken in 1936 they both signed it in the bottom right hand corner.

56. Photographers flocked to the seaside like lemmings. Howe, whom I mentioned a minute ago, was a Louth based photographer but the two major Mablethorpe photographers were Freddie Soar and Derek Camm. Soar had a shop in Victoria Road (the sign is still there today) whilst Camm had a studio in the High Street which he called 'Royal Studios'. On the immediate left of this postcard is a sign saying 'photographs ready in two hours' — a rapid process especially in those days! The building next door to it was aptly nicknamed 'The Old Man's Parliament'!

57. The sort of informal family scenes which appeared in hundreds of photographs taken at the seaside were similar to this. Depicting a happy family group enjoying their picnic on the sands, this is the Havard family from Hertfordshire. From right to left they are: Josephine Havard, Mr. Havard, Mary Hall (wearing a Louth Grammar School hat), Mrs. Havard, Monica Havard, Mrs. Barton and Hilda (Mrs. Havard's sister).

Sand Hills and the Sea, Mablethorpe.

"Empire View" 021-50.

58. Yet another view of the dunes from North End showing Trusthorpe Mill in the far distance. This postcard would have been taken from 'Sea View' car park (just south of what is now 'Mablethorpe Animal Gardens'). In the foreground amongst the clumps of marram grass and sea buckthorn are two little girls sporting chinese parasols which were so popular at the beginning of this century.

3710. TRUSTHORPE MILL, MABLETHORPE

59. Trusthorpe Mill which is now a two story house was reputed to be the highest tower mill in Lincolnshire. John Foster built it in 1885 next door to an old wooden post mill which was demolished in 1901. For a time both mills stood side by side although the mill shown here overshadowed its rickety neighbour and had the wooden mill not been demolished it would probably have fallen down. A present reminder is the bakery which still operates just a short way from the mill.

60. During the Second World War Mablethorpe contributed to the war effort. The town
suffered some bombing and the Clements' Pavillion in Victoria Road was demolished
altogether. In this postcard, which shows a NAAFI waggon outside the YMCA in High
Street at the junction with Waterloo Road, where willing girl guides helped to hand out
the tea. The lady fourth from the right with the gas mask serving the tea is Pat Darby.

61. 'Dear Old Mr Brownlow' who came from Lincoln seemed to be involved with charity work throughout his life collecting pennies, junk or in fact anything he could sell for a few coppers to boost his fund. He is pictured here outside one of the Brownlow bungalows with his pram (the Brownlow bungalows are at the top of Alexandra Road on the right hand side of the grass square). Amongst other things he was given a tea service by the Queen to raise money for his charity and during the Second World War he saved up enough to finance two Spitfires!

62. After the war, Mablethorpe enjoyed a brief respite. This was the view of the 'Pullover' looking down High Street with one noteable difference, the 'Pullover' has been completely concreted.

THE CHALETS AND SOUTH PROMENADE,
MABLETHORPE.

"EMPIRE VIEW", 021·179.

63. Windbreaks appeared on the beach more regularly and a big wheel had been installed. The Coastguard look-out which had been used in the Second World War for spotting enemy planes and ships, resumed normal service. Incidentally during the war, a motor torpedo boat was named HMS 'Mablethorpe', or to be exact M.T.B. No. 45, in recognition of the town.

64. The town's greatest benefactor, as far as education was concerned, was the Reverend James Quarmby (1790-1843). Holding classes first in a private house and then in a granary over a stable he moulded what was later to become known as Mablethorpe primary school. Even when this photograph was taken in the early 1950's, pupils still had to travel to nearby Alford to complete their education. This school was on the corner of High Street opposite the gas works and Miss Powell was the teacher.

3257 Figure 8, Mablethorpe.

65. Butlin's 'figure eight' which is probably better known as a big dipper was dismantled in the late 1930's. The building on the immediate right is Collin's Rock Firm and it was fascinating to see rock being made on the premises. Whilst the café on the right was for a time the site for the 'Water Dodg'ems' but is now a café once more.

66. The Leicester Children's Home was started in 1898 by Lady Rolleston, wife of Sir John Rolleston a well-known Leicester architect. The idea came to her after she had driven through Leicester and noticed the appalling state of some of the underprivileged children. Since that time the home has given sterling service; last year for example, 1,000 children were given a two week break by the sea. There is accommodation for 80 children altogether and the charity which supports them is run by many leading Leicester businessmen. Among the patrons is Englebert Humperdink (the singer) whose brothers and sisters all stayed here. It has been run successfully for the last sixteen years by Mrs. Eagle and the photograph here shows the building which was erected in 1936. During the Second World War the building was camouflaged with green and brown paint and used as an A.R.P. Centre. (An ambulance and air raid warden's post.)

Mablethorpe. South Promenade.　　Nottingham Guardian Photo

67. Mablethorpe has frequently suffered from flooding but nothing on the scale of the 1953 disaster. The first intimation that anything was wrong happend at 5.30 p.m. on the afternoon of 31st January when the sea defences at Sandilands began to crumble. By 7 p.m. great holes had appeared in the sea walls and it was evident that the east coast was in for a rough time. Throughout that night and during the early hours of the following morning the seawater slowly seeped in.

Mablethorpe. Shattered Promenade. Grimsby Telegraph Phot

68. It was the worst disaster within living memory to hit this area and Mablethorpe took the brunt of it. In total forty-three people died that night and at the height of the flooding the water was seven feet deep sweeping over an area of four miles inland. Gales did the worst damage demolishing parts of houses and in some cases complete homes whilst the outlying towns of Alford and Louth served as emergency relief centres.

69. It was estimated that some 750,000 tons of sand had been deposited over the flooded area and when it was all over mopping up operations began. Everyone had to work quickly before the next high tide in mid-February because of the fears of a repetition. The army rushed in troops and 700,000 tons of slag and boulders were transported from Scunthorpe to plug the gaps in the sea wall.

70. Even in the face of adversity the residents of the town did not lose their sense of humour as can be seen in this postcard. This concealed entrance sign which stood in Gibraltar Road has been placed in the gaping hole, which used to be someone's lounge in the Boulevard.

71. If there were heroes on the night of the flood, there were just as many cleaning up the town afterwards. This gang of men were pictured in the Boulevard just a short distance away from the last picture.

72. Media attention quickly centered on Mablethorpe just after the flood. Amongst the many TV, radio and newspaper reporters that descended upon the town was a young, dapper Eamonn Andrews. Pictured here talking to Councillor and Mrs. Richardson, he was compiling material for a sort of 'Down Your Way' programme for the radio.

73. The disaster area was visited by non other than the Duke of Edinburgh, the Duchess of Gloucester and Harold MacMillan. When the new defences had been installed the Duke of Edinburgh came back to inspect them on 14th February 1955. He is pictured here, with the Mayor Reverend Jack Parkinson and in the background are, from left to right: Chief constable Fowkes, inspector Charlie Lewis and sergeant Bray (who did so much courageous work during the flood). Prince Philip was to revisit Mablethorpe on 4th February 1983 on the 30th anniversary of the floods.

74. As if in defiance the local library in promoting John Harris' novel proudly displays posters stating 'The Sea Shall Not Have Them'. It was an apt slogan! In the foreground of this postcard taken in Victoria Road is a group of young girls including Teresa Ripley, Maureen Bogg, Maureen Gooding and Jean Addison — the ponies are called 'Dabbles' and 'Ginger' ('Dabbles' is nearest the camera).

Mablethorpe Caravan Sites at North End.

75. The fifties saw a new type of holiday. For this was the age of the caravan and it was the final nail in the coffin of the railway, which closed in 1960. Many holidaymakers now towed their own private apartments at the back of their cars. This was the view of North End which is now known as Golden Sands.

76. Over the centuries Mablethorpe has experienced a constant battle with the sea. The present defences are strong but who knows what will happen in the future? The sea has always been an uncompromising and unpredictable neighbour. But for me, boyhood memories of Mablethorpe were chiefly visits to the amusement arcades with their penny slot machines (now antiques in their own right, I should think) Donald McGill's saucy seaside postcards and the laughing policeman. Like candy-floss, breathtaking views on the Big Wheel and dodg'em car rides, they remain a blurred vision of a distant past.